canyons. The first scientific investigations of the ruins took place in 1882 under the direction of James Stevenson from the Smithsonian Institution. Initially drawn to the area by the dramatic cliff dwellings, the archeologists eventually realized the prehistoric sites contained an extraordinary record of cultural development.

Evidence of people in Canyon de Chelly reaches back 3500 years and perhaps earlier. As archeologists learn more, this depth of time may increase. Recent investigations have focused on locating and mapping the archeological sites within the monument, while earlier work concentrated on selected excavations. Beginning in the 1920s, archeologist Earl H. Morris recovered a staggering number of artifacts during one field season, enough to fill a boxcar for the American Museum of Natural History. But more important than quantity was the amazing state of preservation.

Stratified deposits in many sites have preserved the artifacts of early inhabitants in nearly pristine condition. Excavators have recovered normally perishable material such as cotton cloth, yucca sandals, and feather blankets. And many masonry walls, built centuries ago, still stand in good condition. Park Service crews had to stabilize only a dozen prehistoric structures within the park. A dry climate, sheltering cliffs, and the watchful eyes of local residents have protected these fragile resources.

Within the monument, the human past is set against a much older geologic past. Most of the rock exposed in the canyon walls represents a single formation, the De Chelly sandstone. More than 230 million years ago winds raked across a vast desert of pure sand, sweeping the rounded grains into dunes. Blowing from the northeast, these ancient winds piled dune upon dune until

the climate shifted. The dunefields became cemented into a sandstone formation 800-feet thick, eventually lying deeply buried under other deposits. Long cycles of uplift and erosion brought the De Chelly sandstone near the surface again.

About 60 million years ago, the formation lay beneath a more resistant rock, the Shinarump conglomerate. Two converging streams, the ancestral Rio de Chelly and Tsaile (say-lee) Creek, meandered across this surface. As the Defiance Plateau began to rise along a 100-mile front, the cutting force of the streams increased. They flowed to the west, maintaining the sinuous curves of their established channels while carving deep gorges into the sloping flank of the plateau.

Snowmelt from the Chuska Mountains and runoff from summer rains continues to feed the Chinle wash. The stream flows through a deeply incised gorge for 27 miles, forming the core of Canyon de Chelly. Its lower end lies near the town of Chinle and its head near Tsaile at the foot of the Chuskas. Tsaile Creek drains Canyon del Muerto, the main tributary gorge that winds for 21 miles before joining De Chelly from the north. Other drainages flow into these, dividing again and again the way veins on a leaf spread from stem to edge.

Only thirty feet deep at its mouth, Canyon de Chelly reaches back into the plateau to gain a depth of twelve hundred feet. At the lower end it receives fewer than ten inches of precipitation during an average year. But an average year rarely occurs. Rainfall fluctuates widely, leaving Navajo farmers to depend more on the geology

Pottery ladle from Antelope House

Tusayan corrugated jar

"Canyon de Chelly is important to the Navajo people," explains park ranger Ailema Benally, herself a Navajo; "they are close to it. This is where their history came from. But they are not locked in the past."

A lumbering, six-wheeled truck heads up the wash of the Chinle wash with a Navajo guide in the driver's seat. In the back sit a group of tourists on their way into the canyon. Sandstone cliffs, wind-laid in ancient crossbedded strata, face each other above a braided stream. In the lower reaches, water flows during spring runoff and after summer rainstorms but sinks below the sands for much of the year. The shifting channel has swept away the talus, the rocky debris at the foot of the cliff, leaving sheer rock to meet the canyon floor at right angles.

Ahead, stone walls follow a ledge set within a curving pocket of sandstone. Centuries-old pictographs, symbols painted in white and red pigments, stipple the wall above the cliff house.

Archeologists have recorded thousands of prehistoric sites within the monument, ranging from isolated campsites to multistoried cliff dwellings. Most remain unexcavated. The earliest solid date, from the 4th century A.D., comes from studying treerings on wood found in a site. But other archeological evidence indicates a human presence 1200 years earlier.

In Canyon de Chelly, the archeological record reflects two major waves of

than the weather. The impermeable Supai formation underlying the De Chelly sandstone creates a high water table and enough soil moisture to grow crops even in dry years.

Canyon de Chelly National Monument is unusual in that it contains not only fine parklands and remnants of the past, but a living community. Archeological evidence places the Navajo people in de Chelly by the mid-to-late 1700s, but oral traditions extend the timeline back by at least half a century. One Navajo story traces the origin of a healing ceremony known as the Nightway Chant to a time when people still inhabited the White House pueblo.

Most Navajo have their permanent homes on the plateau or in town, using the canyon seasonally. About forty families have holdings in Del Muerto and another thirty-five families in de Chelly. Activity slows in the canyon during winter, increasing in tempo when families return to tend their fields during the growing season. Grandparents and young children often live in the canyon when school is out, while other relatives join them in the evenings and on weekends. However, the canyon is not just a place to plant crops or graze livestock.

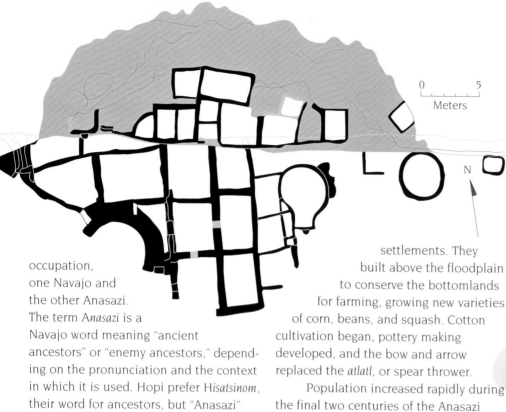

occupation,
one Navajo and
the other Anasazi.
The term *Anasazi* is a
Navajo word meaning "ancient
ancestors" or "enemy ancestors," depend-
ing on the pronunciation and the context
in which it is used. Hopi prefer *Hisatsinom*,
their word for ancestors, but "Anasazi"
remains in common use. Sometimes the
guides call the prehistoric inhabitants
"the old strangers" or "the ones that drifted on" and leave it at that.

The first major period of canyon
settlement spanned fifteen hundred
years from 200 B.C. to A.D. 1300. The early
Anasazi, called Basketmakers, took the
weaving of beautiful baskets and sandals
to levels of skill unmatched by later
generations.

By A.D. 700 the Anasazi pattern of
life had grown distinct enough from the
preceding generations for archeologists
to give it a separate designation. This
new configuration, now known as the
Pueblo period from the Spanish word for
village, was a time of steady population
growth and gathering into compact

settlements. They
built above the floodplain
to conserve the bottomlands
for farming, growing new varieties
of corn, beans, and squash. Cotton
cultivation began, pottery making
developed, and the bow and arrow
replaced the *atlatl*, or spear thrower.

Population increased rapidly during
the final two centuries of the Anasazi
occupation. Smaller settlements consoli-
dated into large pueblos, and the people
took advantage of natural rock shelters.
They often selected south-facing alcoves
to build their homes, locating them
where the low winter sunlight reached.
Temperatures in cliff dwellings range
from 10 to 15 degrees warmer than the
canyon floor.

By the end of the 13th century, the
Anasazi had left Canyon de Chelly. Some
archeologists believe their withdrawal
came when an exploitation of natural
resources led to an environmental crisis.
Others suggest that long-term population growth, coupled with a period of
sustained drought, finally tipped the
balance. Whatever the immediate cause,
the Anasazi migration from Canyon de

Chelley was part of a wider pattern of
resettlement occurring throughout their
homeland.

For the next several hundred years,
Pueblo people made only light use of the
canyon, probably seasonally. Archeologists have found Hopi potsherds
scattered at several dozen sites, but
these are often mixed with Navajo
artifacts. Hopi traditions tell of the Asa
Clan, and others, who lived for a time in
Canyon de Chelly. But whether the
artifacts recovered represent trade, inter-
marriage, or actual settlement remains
unclear.

The Navajo presence marks a
second period of intensive settlement,
but the exact time of arrival has proven
difficult to pin down. The earliest reliable
tree-ring dates for the Navajo in Canyon
de Chelly have come from sites at the
base of Spider Rock. They date from the
late 18th century, when large numbers of
Navajo left their old homeland in what is
now the northwestern corner of New
Mexico. Pressured by frequent Ute
raids, they drifted west of the Chuska
Mountains and may have joined a few
Navajo families already living in Canyon
de Chelly.

For the new arrivals, the topo-
graphic setting provided dependable
water for farming and a natural refuge
from their enemies. Initially the Navajo
located their traditional homes, hogans,
on protected ledges close to the rims for
defense. Before long Canyon de Chelly
gained a reputation as a major stronghold of the Navajo people.

Navajo pictograph of Spanish horsemen in Canyon del Muerto

North Branch

Several miles from the canyon mouth, a break in the cliff wall on the north marks the junction with Canyon del Muerto.

Five miles up this north branch lies Antelope House, an Anasazi pueblo excavated by archeologist Don P. Morris in the 1970s. Beneath a 600-foot cliff stand the stark remnants of a three-story pueblo containing more than 80 rooms. Buried below the prehistoric village, the archeologists found a pithouse from an earlier occupation, extending the record of village growth back to the 8th century.

Floodwaters had destroyed extensive portions of the prehistoric site by the time the archeologists began digging. Located close to the creek channel, the pueblo was vulnerable to flooding. This factor may have played a role in its relative lack of use after 1275, a quarter-century before other major sites.

The Anasazi who lived here depended on farming for the bulk of their subsistence. They grew corn, squash, beans, and cotton on the adjacent bottomlands, but supplemented their crops by hunting animals, such as mule deer, pronghorn antelope, and jackrabbit. From remnants found at Antelope House, researchers know they also gathered a variety of native plants. These included prickly pear cactus, Indian ricegrass, and pinyon pine nuts—their principal wild food source. Using a wide range of resources gave them greater flexibility in responding to an often unpredictable environment.

Above Antelope House, the canyon widens. Broad terraces spread below the red cliffs. At Standing Cow, the profile of a blue-headed cow marks the cliff face. A Navajo artist, Dibé Yazhí (Little Lamb), painted the image of the cow, as well as the graceful antelope figures at Antelope House, more than a century and a half ago.

The sheltered walls of Canyon de Chelly provided ideal locations for pictographs, the figures painted on rock. To make one, the Anasazi took minerals and ground them into pigments. They usually chose white, red, or black, but sometimes vivid yellow, orange, and green. Mixing those with a binder of animal fat or vegetable oils, they applied the paint with brushes made from yucca fiber or animal fur. They also pecked, carved, and abraded petroglyphs into the rock where desert varnish had darkened the surface.

Pictographs often cover the back walls of the canyon's rock shelters. A common figure depicted is the flute player, called *Lahlanhoya* by the Hopi. According to the traditions of the Flute Clan at First Mesa, it represents a clan symbol. Clan members left the glyph on canyon walls to mark the route taken on their long migration from the Place of Emergence.

During their journey they followed a light in the sky, and whenever it disappeared they settled down to wait for its return. In their songs, they refer to one of their stopping places, Canyon de Chelly,

8

Tsegi Overlook

as "the place of running water." While living there, the Hopi saw a light in the west. Again they moved toward it, stopping several times before ending at Walpi on First Mesa.

Members of the Flute Clan have expressed their growing concern with a common misconception. Many people confuse the flute player, they say, with Kokopelli. But Kokopelli, a deity of the Asa Clan, rarely appears in rock art and is never depicted with a flute. Originally a Tano-speaking people from what is now New Mexico, the Asa joined the Hopi in the late 1600s and at one time lived in the Canyon de Chelly area. Traditional representatives for both clans confirm the distinction between the flute player and Kokopelli.

A Navajo pictograph panel at Standing Cow depicts a Spanish military expedition led by Lieutenant Antonio de Narbona in 1805. Soldiers, joined by Opata Indians from Sonora, entered the canyon that winter to retaliate against the Navajo for raiding New Mexican settlements. They also came to capture slaves. In the recorded scene, riders wear heavy winter cloaks and ride slowly by with their muskets ready, searching for the Navajo.

Canyon del Muerto had long been a refuge for the Navajo during times of trouble. When threatened, they withdrew to its isolated buttes and nearly inaccessible ledges, some reached only by hand-and-toe-holds cut in the rock. As Narbona's troops rode into the canyon, the old men, women, and children climbed to a high alcove difficult to see from below. Navajo guide David Wilson recounts one version of what happened next.

At first the soldiers rode past without seeing those concealed above. But then a Navajo woman, angry at her people for not allowing her to marry her cousin, tried to give away their position. "One of the other ladies," says David, "jumped up and grabbed her to pull her down. But both of them fell off. When she screamed, that's when the Spanish looked back. That's when they turned around."

Other Navajo say the woman who called out was a former slave of the Spanish. Unable to restrain herself, she shouted a bitter insult and inadvertently gave away their hiding place.

Narbona divided his party, sending some soldiers back to find a route to the rim. Sharpshooters took up positions above the Indians and began firing into the cave. Shots ricocheted onto those taking shelter below. Unable to escape, more than 100 of the Navajo died from the gunfire in the place since known as Massacre Cave.

More than a century later, archeologist Earl Morris made his first trip into Canyon del Muerto, guided by rancher and self-taught archeologist John Wetherill. He returned the next year, excited by the possibilities, and began excavating. Morris spent several field seasons during the 1920s working deposits at Mummy Cave, Battle Cove, and Big Cave. At the last site, he made an unusual discovery.

Below the cave floor, his crew found two pairs of sandals, beautifully woven in red and black patterns. On top of these lay three shell necklaces and other artifacts, and nearby they uncovered four wooden flutes.

Knocking the dirt from one of these, Morris placed it to his lips and blew. For the first time in a thousand years, the clear notes of the flute reverberated through the rock chamber. Navajo workers paused and listened; a horse raised its head.

"In the weird silence," wrote the archeologist, "it was as if time had been halted in its flight."

M ain Branch

Deep tracks lead up the wash through the main gorge of Canyon de Chelly. Up canyon from the junction with Del Muerto, the braided channel of the Chinle wash

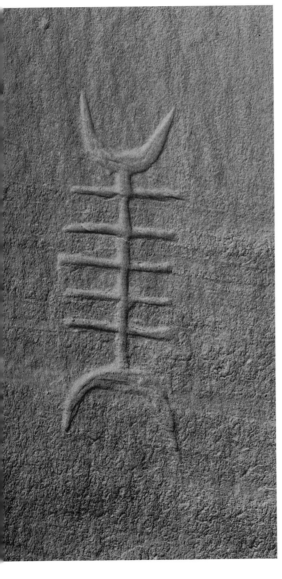

Petroglyph

becomes more restricted in places. On both sides of the stream, cliffs of pure sandstone curve and recurve in deep-set alcoves and massive buttresses.

Suddenly a turn of the canyon discloses a cliff dwelling set in an immense rock face. A sandstone wall sweeps above it in smooth contours for hundreds of feet. Most of the prehistoric masonry blends with the surrounding rock, but a broad band of white highlights the central wall. This is White House, one of largest and best preserved sites in the monument.

Built between A.D. 1060 and 1275, White House consists of two units: the cliff house, with twenty-one rooms, and the pueblo on the canyon floor with about sixty rooms, much of it eaten away by old floods. Built in stepped tiers, the pueblo once reached to within a few feet of the cliff house, providing access to the upper level. Perhaps a dozen families lived at White House when the canyon population reached its peak.

Canyon de Chelly holds deep religious importance for the Navajo people. Traditional Navajo singers continue to recognize the significance of this place. When traveling into the canyon, they stop and pray at various sites. Some consider White House to be the home of the gods, calling it *Kínií ná ígai*, "white streak between the houses."

Descriptions of White House first reached the outside world after American forces took control of New Mexico in 1846. Military commanders

began sending expeditions against the Navajo, attempting to break a generations-old cycle of raiding and retribution. These campaigns, like earlier Spanish efforts, resulted in limited truces and quickly broken treaties. The fighting among Navajo, Utes, and European-Americans continued. A pictograph panel on a wall in Canyon del Muerto records a battle between Ute Indians and the Navajo in 1858. Drawn in somber charcoal tones, the panel shows mounted warriors in feathered headdresses attacking a line of defenders on foot.

Troops withdrew from the frontier at the outbreak of the Civil War, abandoning many outposts, and the raiding increased. When Brigadier General James H. Carleton took command, he ordered the legendary scout Kit Carson into the field. His mission was to destroy the Navajo subsistence base and force a final surrender.

In 1864, Colonel Carson led a contingent of New Mexican volunteers and Ute scouts to Canyon de Chelly. Bitter cold and deep snows aided the soldiers. Cavalry detachments traversed both arms of the canyon, penetrating the Navajo stronghold.

"Kit Carson and his troops came here," said guide David Wilson. "They burned all the hogans they saw here, and they killed lots of livestock. It was in the winter time. Lots of people froze and a lot of people starved. So finally they gave up."

The Navajo began to surrender by the hundreds when they learned they

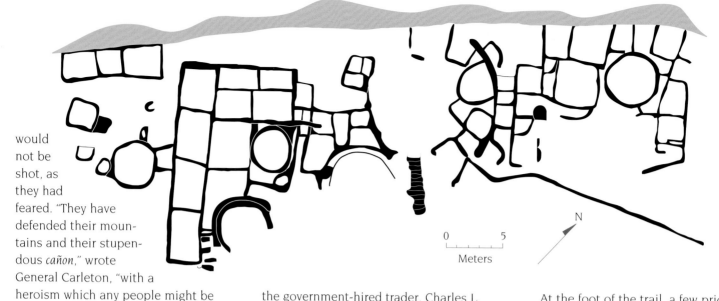

would not be shot, as they had feared. "They have defended their mountains and their stupendous *cañon*," wrote General Carleton, "with a heroism which any people might be proud to emulate."

Uprooted from their homeland, many died on the long journey to Fort Sumner in eastern New Mexico. By March 1865, the military had confined 9000 Navajo on a desolate reservation there and attempted to transform them into a settled, village-dwelling people. The experiment failed. But during those times of suffering, the Navajo forged a new identity. They began to see themselves as a single people, politically united, instead of a patchwork of clans and local bands. In 1868, government officials allowed the Navajo to return to their own country where they struggled to rebuild their lives.

Traders began to enter the Navajo country soon after the return from Fort Sumner. The first documented trader at Canyon de Chelly, known by his Navajo name of Nakai Yazhi, pitched a tent near the canyon mouth in 1882. Within a few years, others followed. Garcia's trading post opened in 1886 and the Day family began trading in 1902. A year later,

the government-hired trader, Charles L. Day, became Canyon de Chelly's first custodian. Earning a salary of $10 a month, he was expected to protect the canyon's archeological resources from the growing threat of looters.

Eventually acquired by Cozy McSparron, the trading post began to shift its focus to accommodating tourists and evolved into today's Thunderbird Lodge.

From the rim the trail to White House descends 550 feet, cutting through the crossbedded De Chelly sandstone. Hikers can make the 2.5-mile round-trip without a guide, passing through a variety of plant communities. The trailhead lies in the pinyon-juniper woodland covering the plateau. These tough, spare trees can survive both summer drought and winter cold. Prickly pear cactus, cholla, rabbitbrush, and snakeweed grow among them. Leaving the rim, the trail descends the face of the canyon, winding past Gambel oak, juniper, and box elder on the terraces below.

At the foot of the trail, a few prickly pear grow on the dirt roof of a notched-log hogan, a traditional Navajo home. Hogans, often octagonal, always face the rising sun. Stands of Fremont cottonwood and coyote willow, both native species, border the Chinle wash. Nearby grow thickets of Russian olive and tamarisk, which were introduced for erosion control. Crews made regular plantings of these trees to protect archeological sites and Navajo homesteads from floods. Eventually vegetation became so thick near White House in the mid-1940s that crews cut it back when the trees threatened to damage the site.

Dark tendrils of desert varnish streak the cliff above the prehistoric village. Bacteria live on the rock where runoff provides some moisture. These microbes take dust from the air and digest it, fixing manganese and other minerals to the wall.

Farther up the canyon stands the legendary Spider Rock, *Tsé na' ashje'ii.* The solitary pinnacle divides into two summits with the highest reaching 800

Antelope House in Canyon del Muerto

into fabrics. Deposits at Antelope House held cotton seeds, stalks, and bolls; weaving tools; and even the finished cotton fabric. While excavating across the canyon at Battle Cove, archeologist Earl Morris found what he called the Tomb of the Weaver.

Standing on the rim overlooking Spider Rock, Chauncey Neboyia continued. "They say Spider Woman used to live on top of Spider Rock. Spider Woman is the holiest person. They say Spider Woman made twelve gods: One god for the earth, one god for the sky, the moon, sun, and stars, and all these plants and animals, humans, and rains.

"In the early morning," Neboyia added, "all these Holy People that live in this area see a rainbow right here. It's the most sacred part of the canyon."

feet above the streambed. Face Rock stands across the wash from it, and Monument Canyon, a major tributary gorge, joins the main gorge from the south. The Chinle wash runs along the slickrock slopes at the foot of the cliffs. Farther up the wash, where the canyon reaches its greatest depth, talus slopes crowd the floor.

"Spider Rock," Guide Chauncey Neboyia said slowly, speaking English with a Navajo cadence. "Home of Spider Woman."

Neboyia stood on the rim of Canyon de Chelly looking across the deep vista at the spire. Light struck the west face, throwing a long shadow against the cliffs. A dog barked in the distance, the sound swallowed in the depths of the gorge.

"Nobody could see the Spider Woman," he said. "They could just feel her. Every morning when she gets up, she prays for a rainbow across to the other side. She had heard the Lizard Clan people who lived there grinding corn and wanted to join them. So Spider Woman travels on the rainbow; she goes over to the other side." He paused before adding, "Spider Woman taught the Navajo people how to weave."

Spanish officials described the Navajo as a people who wove blankets from wool and also from the cotton they grew. Weaving has a long history at Canyon de Chelly. Evidence unearthed at Antelope House suggests the region became a cotton textile center during Anasazi times. The Anasazi grew cotton, spun it into yarn, and wove it

A herd of goats on a canyon path